My

Wellness

TRACKER

A JOURNAL TO HELP YOU MAP OUT AND MAXIMIZE YOUR WELL-BEING

ANNA BARNES

MY WELLNESS TRACKER

An Hachette UK Company
www.hachette.co.uk

Vie Books, an imprint of Summersdale Publishers Ltd
Part of Octopus Publishing Group Limited
Carmelite House
50 Victoria Embankment
LONDON
EC4Y 0DZ
UK

www.summersdale.com

Printed and bound in the Czech Republic

ISBN: 978-1-78783-638-9

Substantial discounts on bulk quantities of Summersdale books are available to corporations, professional associations and other organizations. For details contact general enquiries: telephone: +44 (0) 1243 771107 or email: enquiries@summersdale.com.

Disclaimer

This book is not intended as a substitute for the medical advice of a doctor or physician. If you are experiencing problems with your health, it is always best to follow the advice of a medical professional.

Nurturing yourself is not selfish – it's essential to your survival and well-being.

RENÉE PETERSON TRUDEAU

Introduction

We can all feel out of balance sometimes and it's not always easy to pinpoint why. When we spend so much of our time preoccupied by the demands and responsibilities of daily life, it's easy to let our mental and physical health slip down on our list of priorities.

This journal is here to offer you guidance and support on your path to wellness. Taking a holistic approach to well-being, this tracker allows you to record your mood, sleep, food, drink and exercise over the course of a year, to help you better understand the patterns in your health and happiness.

With monthly well-being themes to explore – on topics including motivation, self-care, mindfulness and creativity – as well as uplifting quotes and affirmations, this book will help to inspire and encourage you on your wellness journey. By uncovering the links between your mind and your mood, you'll soon realize that your wellness is within your control.

Read on to begin your journey…

Wellness Tracker

On each day this month, colour in one shape
according to how you feel.

KEY

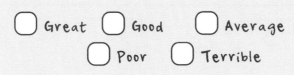

Great   Good   Average
Poor   Terrible

I am open to
change and
willing to evolve

Top Tips

BUILDING MOTIVATION

Take the Pressure Off

January often brings with it a feeling of change or resolution, inspiring many of us to set ourselves plenty of challenges for the New Year. On the other hand, there are some years we enter into feeling rather less motivated, struggling to build up any energy or enthusiasm. Whichever of these two categories we fall into, we could be doing ourselves a disservice; either we burn ourselves out by pushing ourselves to the limit, or we feel low because we've failed to make the most of what feels like a "fresh start". This year, take the pressure off and free yourself from expectation. Take each day as it comes and set wellness as your top priority; everything else will follow.

Do More of What You Love

Set aside some time to reflect on the year that has passed, and think about what it was that really made you happy and made you feel your best. Give yourself permission to create more time for what you love this year; in doing so, you will feel more positive and inspired, and have more energy to expend on other things.

Exercise tracker

Use this page to log your levels of
activity over this month.

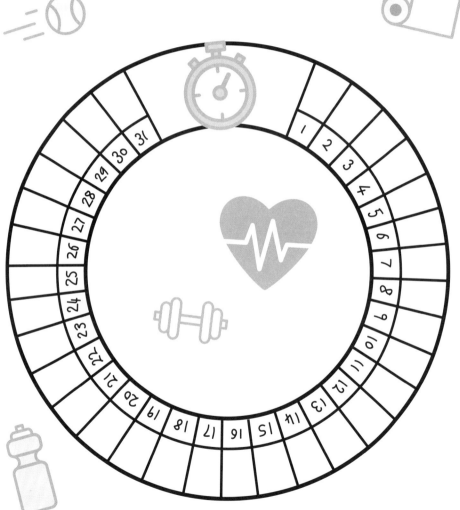

- ⬜ ACTIVE
- ⬜ MODERATELY ACTIVE
- ⬜ REST DAY

Motivation comes
from working on things
we care about.

SHERYL SANDBERG

Five a Day Tracker

Each apple = one of your five
fruits or vegetables a day

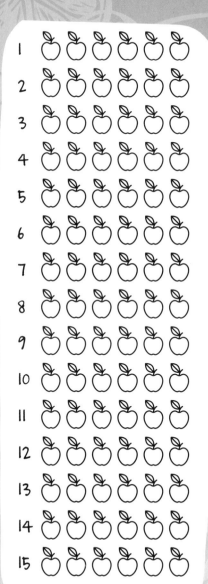

1
2
3
4
5
6
7
8
9
10
11
12
13
14
15

16
17
18
19
20
21
22
23
24
25
26
27
28
29
30
31

Water Tracker

One drop = one glass (400 ml)

1 ○○○○○○○○
2 ○○○○○○○○
3 ○○○○○○○○
4 ○○○○○○○○
5 ○○○○○○○○
6 ○○○○○○○○
7 ○○○○○○○○
8 ○○○○○○○○
9 ○○○○○○○○
10 ○○○○○○○○
11 ○○○○○○○○
12 ○○○○○○○○
13 ○○○○○○○○
14 ○○○○○○○○
15 ○○○○○○○○

16 ○○○○○○○○
17 ○○○○○○○○
18 ○○○○○○○○
19 ○○○○○○○○
20 ○○○○○○○○
21 ○○○○○○○○
22 ○○○○○○○○
23 ○○○○○○○○
24 ○○○○○○○○
25 ○○○○○○○○
26 ○○○○○○○○
27 ○○○○○○○○
28 ○○○○○○○○
29 ○○○○○○○○
30 ○○○○○○○○
31 ○○○○○○○○

Stress Tracker

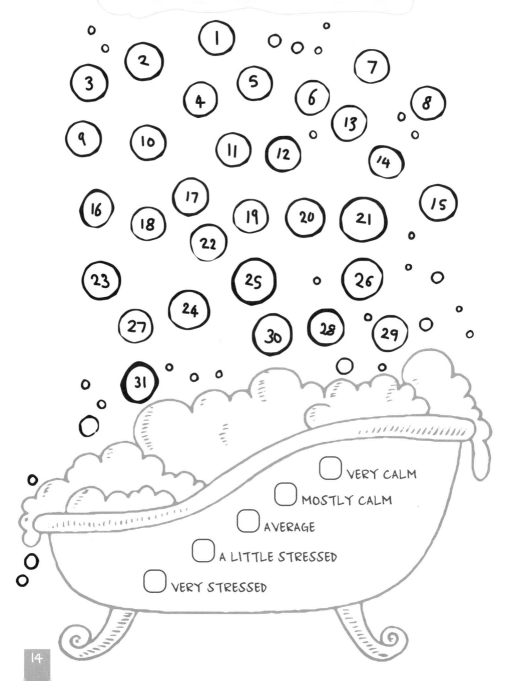

- [ ] VERY CALM
- [ ] MOSTLY CALM
- [ ] AVERAGE
- [ ] A LITTLE STRESSED
- [ ] VERY STRESSED

Working Out
My Worries

Use this page to write down some of the things that you are worried about this month. Then think about ways you could overcome your worries, and write down some ideas you'd like to try out.

Things I'm worried about

_____

_____

_____

_____

How to overcome them

_____

_____

_____

_____

Sleep Tracker

- ☐ FOUR HOURS OR FEWER ☐ FIVE HOURS ☐ SIX HOURS
- ☐ SEVEN HOURS ☐ EIGHT HOURS ☐ NINE HOURS OR MORE

Calm Activity

INSPIRATIONAL TOP FIVE

Draw a picture of the top five things that
inspire you at the moment.

Reflect: can you make any of the things that
inspire you a more prominent feature of your daily
routine, to help keep you motivated?

Wellness tracker

On each day this month, colour in one shape
according to how you feel.

KEY

◯ Great ◯ Good ◯ Average
◯ Poor ◯ Terrible

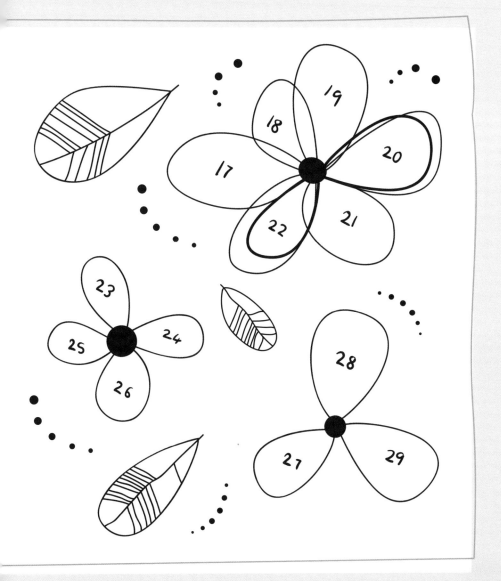

I am worthy
of self-love and I
recognize the necessity
of self-care

Top Tips

DEVELOPING SELF-CARE

Self-Care as a Necessity

Though most of us might view self-care as an indulgence, taking time out of our schedules to nourish and look after ourselves is critical to our well-being. By finding time to nurture ourselves, we create space for the mind and the body to rest and replenish; without it, we would soon burn out – leaving us unable to do all the other tasks on our to-do list!

Finding Time for Self-Care

Here are some ideas to help you find a few moments of self-care in your day:

- Claim at least 15 minutes of your day to do something that you enjoy. This could be as simple as a mindful walk, reading a book, sitting down with a cup of tea or having a hot shower with your favourite body wash.

- Pause for five minutes every day and notice what is going on within your body and mind; notice any tension you are carrying around and take a few moments to stretch and relax.

- If you find yourself unable to cope with the demands in your day, consider what you could cut out. Practise setting boundaries and allow yourself the opportunity to say "no" when you need to.

Exercise tracker

Use this page to log your levels of
activity over this month.

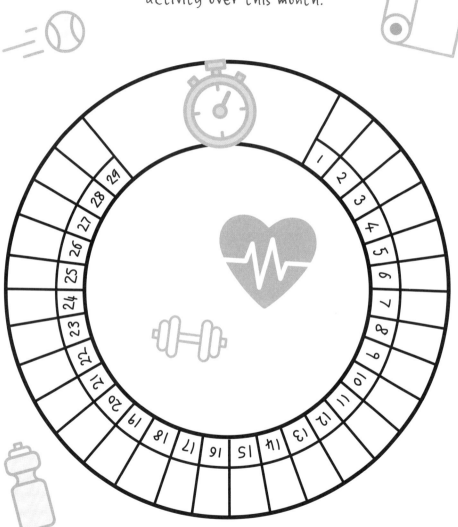

⃝ ACTIVE   ⃝ MODERATELY ACTIVE   ⃝ REST DAY

I've been searching for ways to heal myself, and I've found that kindness is the best way.

LADY GAGA

Five A Day Tracker

Each apple = one of your five
fruits or vegetables a day

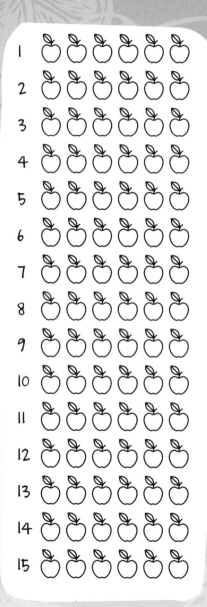

Water Tracker

One drop = one glass (400 ml)

1 ⬠ ⬠ ⬠ ⬠ ⬠ ⬠ ⬠ ⬠
2 ⬠ ⬠ ⬠ ⬠ ⬠ ⬠ ⬠ ⬠
3 ⬠ ⬠ ⬠ ⬠ ⬠ ⬠ ⬠ ⬠
4 ⬠ ⬠ ⬠ ⬠ ⬠ ⬠ ⬠ ⬠
5 ⬠ ⬠ ⬠ ⬠ ⬠ ⬠ ⬠ ⬠
6 ⬠ ⬠ ⬠ ⬠ ⬠ ⬠ ⬠ ⬠
7 ⬠ ⬠ ⬠ ⬠ ⬠ ⬠ ⬠ ⬠
8 ⬠ ⬠ ⬠ ⬠ ⬠ ⬠ ⬠ ⬠
9 ⬠ ⬠ ⬠ ⬠ ⬠ ⬠ ⬠ ⬠
10 ⬠ ⬠ ⬠ ⬠ ⬠ ⬠ ⬠ ⬠
11 ⬠ ⬠ ⬠ ⬠ ⬠ ⬠ ⬠ ⬠
12 ⬠ ⬠ ⬠ ⬠ ⬠ ⬠ ⬠ ⬠
13 ⬠ ⬠ ⬠ ⬠ ⬠ ⬠ ⬠ ⬠
14 ⬠ ⬠ ⬠ ⬠ ⬠ ⬠ ⬠ ⬠
15 ⬠ ⬠ ⬠ ⬠ ⬠ ⬠ ⬠ ⬠

16 ⬠ ⬠ ⬠ ⬠ ⬠ ⬠ ⬠ ⬠
17 ⬠ ⬠ ⬠ ⬠ ⬠ ⬠ ⬠ ⬠
18 ⬠ ⬠ ⬠ ⬠ ⬠ ⬠ ⬠ ⬠
19 ⬠ ⬠ ⬠ ⬠ ⬠ ⬠ ⬠ ⬠
20 ⬠ ⬠ ⬠ ⬠ ⬠ ⬠ ⬠ ⬠
21 ⬠ ⬠ ⬠ ⬠ ⬠ ⬠ ⬠ ⬠
22 ⬠ ⬠ ⬠ ⬠ ⬠ ⬠ ⬠ ⬠
23 ⬠ ⬠ ⬠ ⬠ ⬠ ⬠ ⬠ ⬠
24 ⬠ ⬠ ⬠ ⬠ ⬠ ⬠ ⬠ ⬠
25 ⬠ ⬠ ⬠ ⬠ ⬠ ⬠ ⬠ ⬠
26 ⬠ ⬠ ⬠ ⬠ ⬠ ⬠ ⬠ ⬠
27 ⬠ ⬠ ⬠ ⬠ ⬠ ⬠ ⬠ ⬠
28 ⬠ ⬠ ⬠ ⬠ ⬠ ⬠ ⬠ ⬠
29 ⬠ ⬠ ⬠ ⬠ ⬠ ⬠ ⬠ ⬠

Stress Tracker

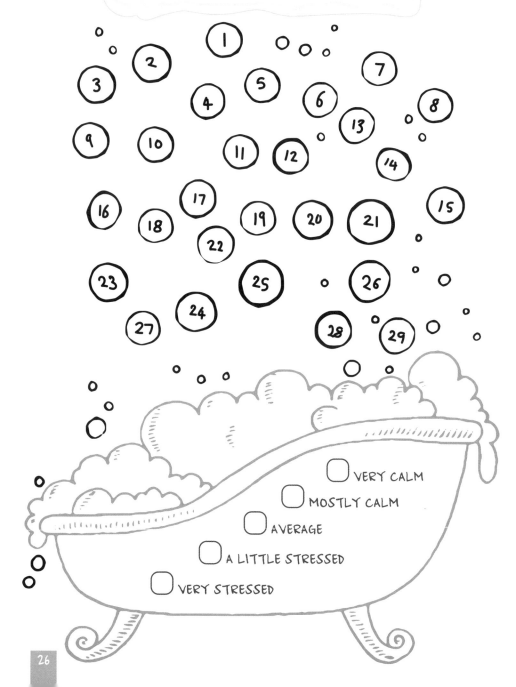

1 2 3 4 5 6 7 8 9 10 11 12 13 14 15 16 17 18 19 20 21 22 23 24 25 26 27 28 29

☐ VERY CALM
☐ MOSTLY CALM
☐ AVERAGE
☐ A LITTLE STRESSED
☐ VERY STRESSED

Working Out My Worries

Use this page to write down some of the things that you are worried about this month. Then think about ways you could overcome your worries, and write down some ideas you'd like to try out.

Things I'm worried about

_____

_____

_____

_____

How to overcome them

_____

_____

_____

_____

Sleep Tracker

- ☐ FOUR HOURS OR FEWER ☐ FIVE HOURS ☐ SIX HOURS
- ☐ SEVEN HOURS ☐ EIGHT HOURS ☐ NINE HOURS OR MORE

Calm Activity

SELF-CARE LIST

In each heart below, list one thing that feels like a nurturing act of self-care. Work your way through the list this month.

Wellness tracker

On each day this month, colour in one shape
according to how you feel.

KEY

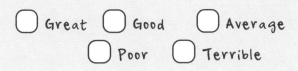

◯ Great ◯ Good ◯ Average
◯ Poor ◯ Terrible

All the wisdom
I could ever need is
already inside me,
guiding me in
this moment

Top Tips

PRACTISING MINDFULNESS

Focus on Each Moment

Feeling overwhelmed is normal – especially in today's society, where we so often have to grapple with endless tasks and deadlines at work and at home. It is important to remember that no matter how long our to-do list is, we only ever have the present moment to work with. "Now" is the only time that exists – anything before is gone, and anything after hasn't happened yet. So, deal with your tasks from moment to moment, and only do the best you can.

Mindful Breathing

Sometimes it helps to practise mindful breathing. Follow these three simple steps to find calm, and repeat as often needed:

- Sit comfortably and close your eyes. Begin to notice the rhythm of your breathing.

- Inhale for a count of six seconds, and pay attention to the rising of your chest. Pause and hold your breath for four seconds.

- Exhale for a count of eight seconds, and notice your chest slowly falling. Take a moment to notice how you feel, and listen to the noises that surround you.

Exercise tracker

Use this page to log your levels of
activity over this month.

◯ ACTIVE   ◯ MODERATELY ACTIVE   ◯ REST DAY

Breathe. Let go. And
remind yourself that this
very moment is the only one
you know you have for sure.

OPRAH WINFREY

Five A Day Tracker

Each apple = one of your five
fruits or vegetables a day

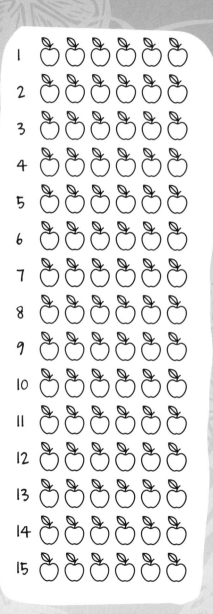

Water Tracker

One drop = one glass (400 ml)

1 ○○○○○○○○
2 ○○○○○○○○
3 ○○○○○○○○
4 ○○○○○○○○
5 ○○○○○○○○
6 ○○○○○○○○
7 ○○○○○○○○
8 ○○○○○○○○
9 ○○○○○○○○
10 ○○○○○○○○
11 ○○○○○○○○
12 ○○○○○○○○
13 ○○○○○○○○
14 ○○○○○○○○
15 ○○○○○○○○

16 ○○○○○○○○
17 ○○○○○○○○
18 ○○○○○○○○
19 ○○○○○○○○
20 ○○○○○○○○
21 ○○○○○○○○
22 ○○○○○○○○
23 ○○○○○○○○
24 ○○○○○○○○
25 ○○○○○○○○
26 ○○○○○○○○
27 ○○○○○○○○
28 ○○○○○○○○
29 ○○○○○○○○
30 ○○○○○○○○
31 ○○○○○○○○

Stress Tracker

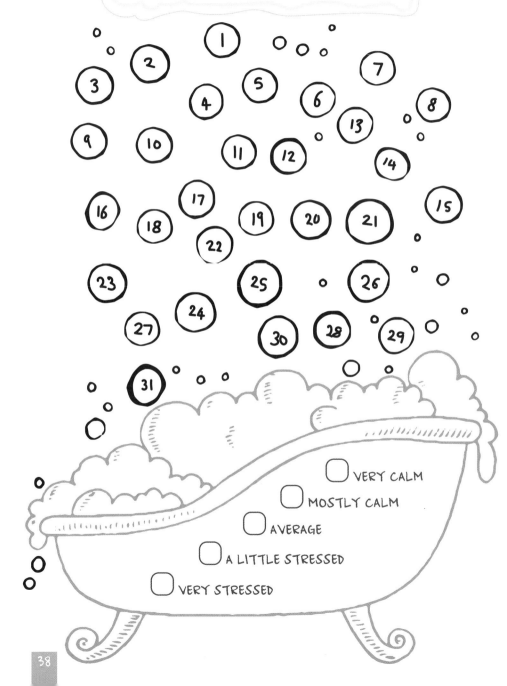

VERY CALM

MOSTLY CALM

AVERAGE

A LITTLE STRESSED

VERY STRESSED

Working Out My Worries

Use this page to write down some of the things that you are worried about this month. Then think about ways you could overcome your worries, and write down some ideas you'd like to try out.

Things I'm worried about

_____

_____

_____

_____

How to overcome them

_____

_____

_____

_____

Sleep Tracker

☐ FOUR HOURS OR FEWER ☐ FIVE HOURS ☐ SIX HOURS

☐ SEVEN HOURS ☐ EIGHT HOURS ☐ NINE HOURS OR MORE

Calm Activity

MINDFULNESS MAZE

When we spend time being mindful, we sometimes find that our new mindset allows us to think about our problems in new ways. Can you find your way to the heart below in our mindfulness maze?

Wellness tracker

On each day this month, colour in one shape
according to how you feel.

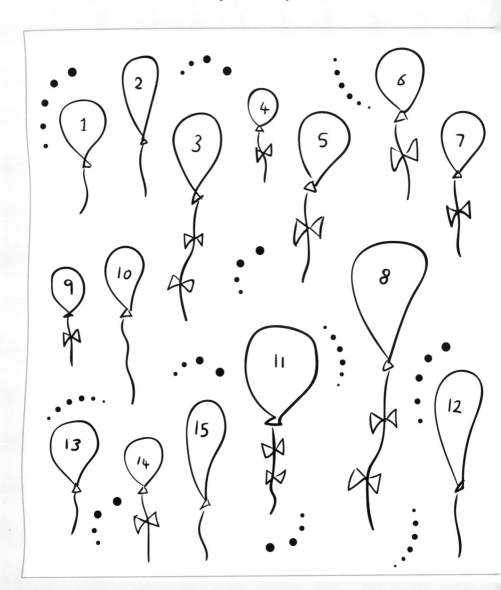

KEY

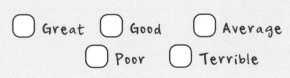

◯ Great ◯ Good ◯ Average

◯ Poor ◯ Terrible

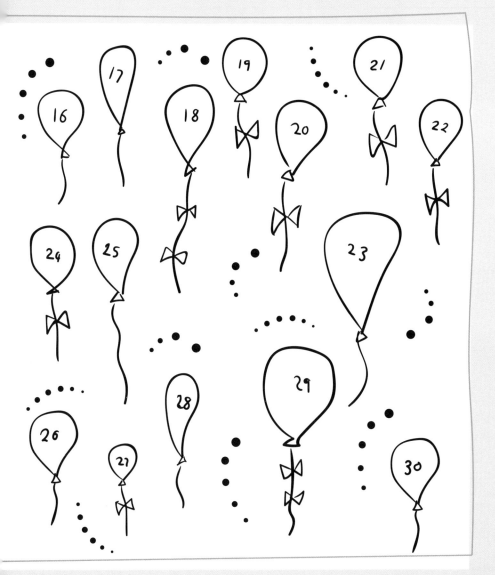

I embrace the
possibilities of
each moment

Top Tips

EMBRACING CHANGE

Be Adaptable

Change is part of life, and it's important that we stay open and adaptable to the changes that each day, month and year brings. The more that we embrace the unpredictability of each moment, the happier we will find ourselves in new situations.

Feel Yourself Grow

Change is all about taking on new challenges and opening your mind to new possibilities. See change as a chance to grow and learn – an opportunity to meet new people and explore new places. We never know what amazing things might come from stepping into the unknown. Even if the place you enter into isn't as good as what you had before, at least you tried it out.

Give Yourself Time

Even though there's excitement in new possibilities, it's not always easy to jump into everything headfirst. Make sure you give yourself permission to adjust to change, and look after your needs in the process. It's important that you prioritize your well-being so that you continue to grow.

Exercise tracker

Use this page to log your levels of
activity over this month.

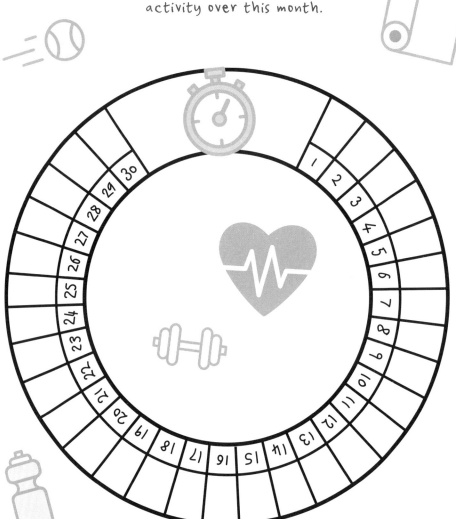

○ ACTIVE   ○ MODERATELY ACTIVE   ○ REST DAY

If you can dream it,
you can do it.

TOM FITZGERALD

Five A Day Tracker

Each apple = one of your five
fruits or vegetables a day

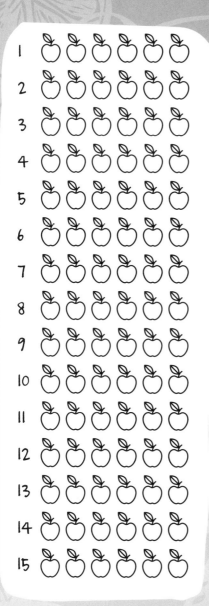

1
2
3
4
5
6
7
8
9
10
11
12
13
14
15

16
17
18
19
20
21
22
23
24
25
26
27
28
29
30

Water Tracker

One drop = one glass (400 ml)

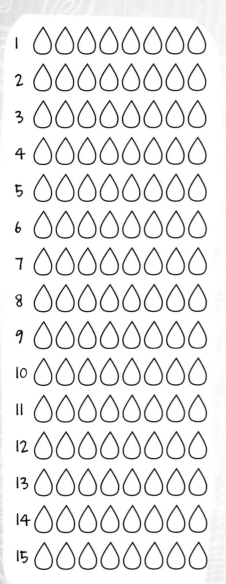

1 ⬭⬭⬭⬭⬭⬭⬭⬭	16 ⬭⬭⬭⬭⬭⬭⬭⬭
2 ⬭⬭⬭⬭⬭⬭⬭⬭	17 ⬭⬭⬭⬭⬭⬭⬭⬭
3 ⬭⬭⬭⬭⬭⬭⬭⬭	18 ⬭⬭⬭⬭⬭⬭⬭⬭
4 ⬭⬭⬭⬭⬭⬭⬭⬭	19 ⬭⬭⬭⬭⬭⬭⬭⬭
5 ⬭⬭⬭⬭⬭⬭⬭⬭	20 ⬭⬭⬭⬭⬭⬭⬭⬭
6 ⬭⬭⬭⬭⬭⬭⬭⬭	21 ⬭⬭⬭⬭⬭⬭⬭⬭
7 ⬭⬭⬭⬭⬭⬭⬭⬭	22 ⬭⬭⬭⬭⬭⬭⬭⬭
8 ⬭⬭⬭⬭⬭⬭⬭⬭	23 ⬭⬭⬭⬭⬭⬭⬭⬭
9 ⬭⬭⬭⬭⬭⬭⬭⬭	24 ⬭⬭⬭⬭⬭⬭⬭⬭
10 ⬭⬭⬭⬭⬭⬭⬭⬭	25 ⬭⬭⬭⬭⬭⬭⬭⬭
11 ⬭⬭⬭⬭⬭⬭⬭⬭	26 ⬭⬭⬭⬭⬭⬭⬭⬭
12 ⬭⬭⬭⬭⬭⬭⬭⬭	27 ⬭⬭⬭⬭⬭⬭⬭⬭
13 ⬭⬭⬭⬭⬭⬭⬭⬭	28 ⬭⬭⬭⬭⬭⬭⬭⬭
14 ⬭⬭⬭⬭⬭⬭⬭⬭	29 ⬭⬭⬭⬭⬭⬭⬭⬭
15 ⬭⬭⬭⬭⬭⬭⬭⬭	30 ⬭⬭⬭⬭⬭⬭⬭⬭

Stress Tracker

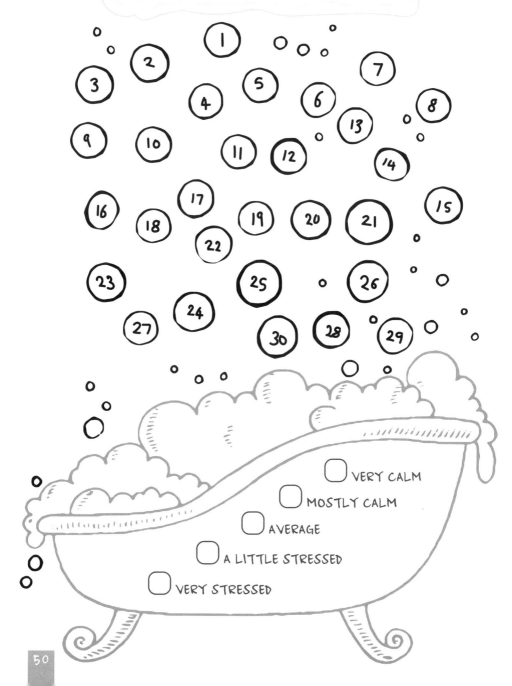

1 2 3 4 5 6 7 8 9 10 11 12 13 14 15 16 17 18 19 20 21 22 23 24 25 26 27 28 29 30

☐ VERY CALM
☐ MOSTLY CALM
☐ AVERAGE
☐ A LITTLE STRESSED
☐ VERY STRESSED

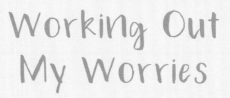

Working Out My Worries

Use this page to write down some of the things that you are worried about this month. Then think about ways you could overcome your worries, and write down some ideas you'd like to try out.

Things I'm worried about

_____

_____

_____

_____

How to overcome them

_____

_____

_____

_____

Sleep Tracker

⬭ FOUR HOURS OR FEWER ⬭ FIVE HOURS ⬭ SIX HOURS
⬭ SEVEN HOURS ⬭ EIGHT HOURS ⬭ NINE HOURS OR MORE

Calm Activity

CONFIDENCE PLAYLIST

Create a playlist of songs that help you
to feel confident and capable.

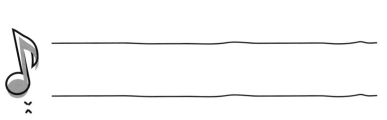

**My top five confidence
songs are:**

_____

_____

_____

_____

_____

Wellness tracker

On each day this month, colour in one shape
according to how you feel.

KEY

◯ Great ◯ Good ◯ Average
◯ Poor ◯ Terrible

My spirit
is nourished by
spending time
in nature

Top Tips

FINDING CALM IN NATURE

Spend Time Outside

Being in nature brings a sense of peace to many of us, and the more time we can spend outside, the better it is for our well-being. In fact, a study by the UK charity Mind showed that 95 per cent of participants felt happier after spending time outside, changing their moods from depressed, stressed and anxious to calm and balanced. When we reconnect to the natural world, it tends to relax us, as well as encouraging us to be more mindful. This is particularly useful when we are feeling anxious and preoccupied by unwanted thoughts, as it can help us take our minds off the uncertainty of the future.

Pay Attention to Your Surroundings

Next time you are feeling anxious, try heading to your nearest outdoor space (even if it's a square of grass just outside your home) and removing your shoes and socks. Stand barefoot in the grass for five minutes and focus on the feeling of the ground beneath your feet. As you do this, listen to what is going on around you. Focus on the sounds and smells of nature, and allow them to fill your mind. Notice how this makes you feel.

Exercise tracker

Use this page to log your levels of
activity over this month.

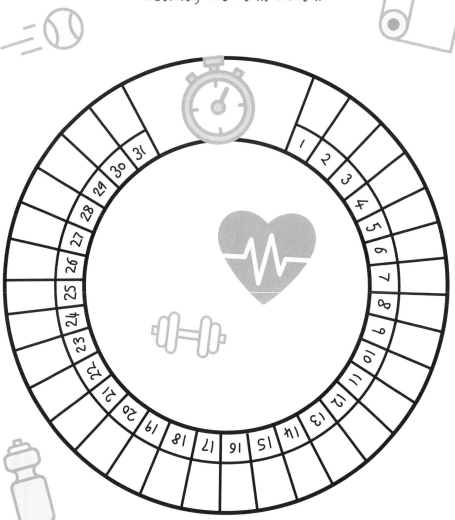

⬭ ACTIVE   ⬭ MODERATELY ACTIVE   ⬭ REST DAY

When you take a flower
in your hand and really
look at it, it's your world
for the moment.

GEORGIA O'KEEFFE

Five A Day Tracker

Each apple = one of your five
fruits or vegetables a day

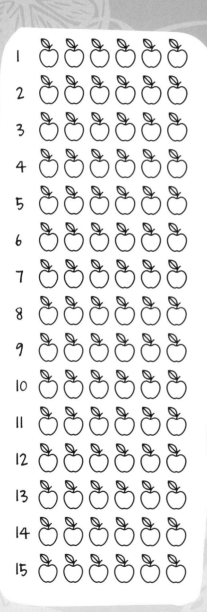

Water Tracker

One drop = one glass (400 ml)

1 ◊◊◊◊◊◊◊◊
2 ◊◊◊◊◊◊◊◊
3 ◊◊◊◊◊◊◊◊
4 ◊◊◊◊◊◊◊◊
5 ◊◊◊◊◊◊◊◊
6 ◊◊◊◊◊◊◊◊
7 ◊◊◊◊◊◊◊◊
8 ◊◊◊◊◊◊◊◊
9 ◊◊◊◊◊◊◊◊
10 ◊◊◊◊◊◊◊◊
11 ◊◊◊◊◊◊◊◊
12 ◊◊◊◊◊◊◊◊
13 ◊◊◊◊◊◊◊◊
14 ◊◊◊◊◊◊◊◊
15 ◊◊◊◊◊◊◊◊

16 ◊◊◊◊◊◊◊◊
17 ◊◊◊◊◊◊◊◊
18 ◊◊◊◊◊◊◊◊
19 ◊◊◊◊◊◊◊◊
20 ◊◊◊◊◊◊◊◊
21 ◊◊◊◊◊◊◊◊
22 ◊◊◊◊◊◊◊◊
23 ◊◊◊◊◊◊◊◊
24 ◊◊◊◊◊◊◊◊
25 ◊◊◊◊◊◊◊◊
26 ◊◊◊◊◊◊◊◊
27 ◊◊◊◊◊◊◊◊
28 ◊◊◊◊◊◊◊◊
29 ◊◊◊◊◊◊◊◊
30 ◊◊◊◊◊◊◊◊
31 ◊◊◊◊◊◊◊◊

Stress Tracker

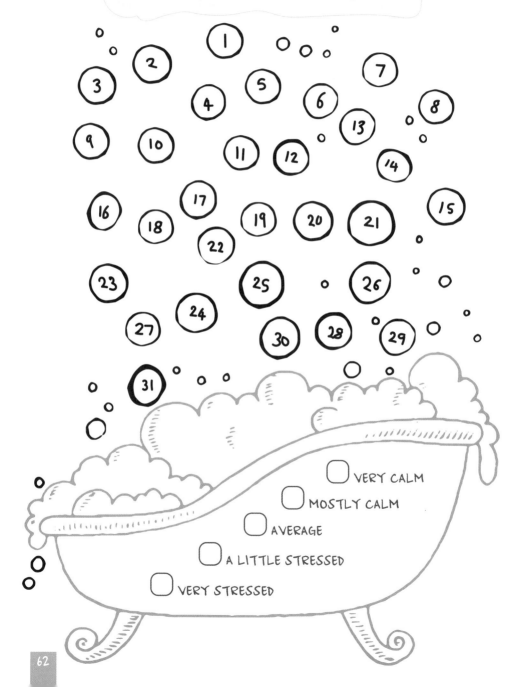

- VERY CALM
- MOSTLY CALM
- AVERAGE
- A LITTLE STRESSED
- VERY STRESSED

Working Out My Worries

Use this page to write down some of the things that you are worried about this month. Then think about ways you could overcome your worries, and write down some ideas you'd like to try out.

Things I'm worried about

_____

_____

_____

_____

How to overcome them

_____

_____

_____

_____

Sleep Tracker

○ FOUR HOURS OR FEWER   ○ FIVE HOURS   ○ SIX HOURS

○ SEVEN HOURS   ○ EIGHT HOURS   ○ NINE HOURS OR MORE

Calm Activity

SIMPLE SKETCHING

Each time you go into nature this month, take photos
of some of the objects you find — it could be a verdant
leaf, a vibrant flower or a beautiful seashell. On this
page, sketch out some of the items you've captured to
remind you of the wonder of nature.

Wellness tracker

On each day this month, colour in one shape
according to how you feel.

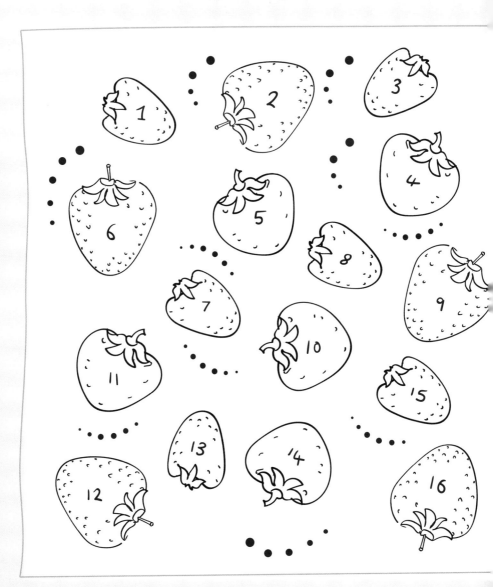

KEY

☐ Great ☐ Good ☐ Average
☐ Poor ☐ Terrible

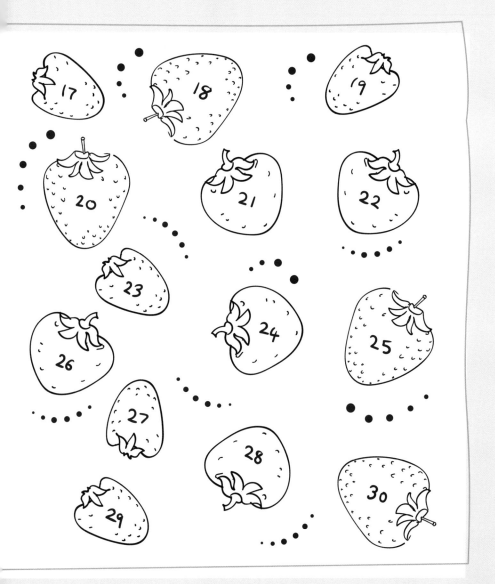

I love myself completely and I embrace my uniqueness

Top Tips

DEVELOPING SELF-LOVE

Start with a Positive

Self-love can be challenging for some of us, and cycles of negative thinking can lead to poor mental well-being. To try to combat negative self-talk, start each day by telling yourself something positive. You could compliment yourself on how well you cared for yourself the previous day or how well you look after a good night's rest. Either way, allow it to set the tone for the rest of your day.

Stop the Comparisons

Comparing yourself to other people never brings joy or fulfilment. Not only can you not fairly compare yourself to others based on what you see of their life (which, most often, is only a highlight reel), but you also cannot compare one unique individual to another. No one is exactly the same as you, and no one is on the same course in their life. Allow yourself to accept your own situation, and work on yourself *for* yourself – not to match up to anyone around you.

Find Gratitude

Write down three things you are grateful for every day. No matter how small, always remember to count your blessings. You'll find this practice helps you to truly appreciate your incredible mind and body.

Exercise tracker

Use this page to log your levels of
activity over this month.

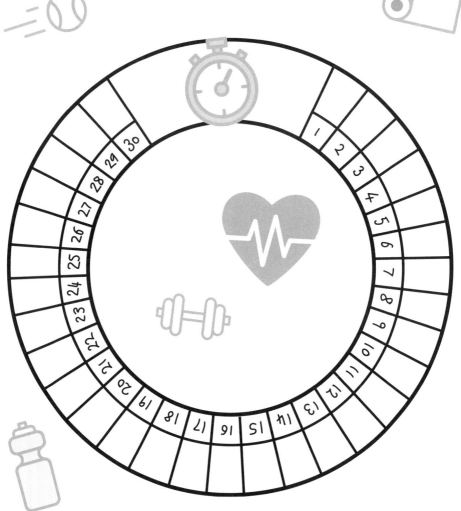

○ ACTIVE   ○ MODERATELY ACTIVE   ○ REST DAY

The minute you learn to
love yourself, you would
not want to be anyone else.

RIHANNA

Five A Day Tracker

Each apple = one of your five
fruits or vegetables a day

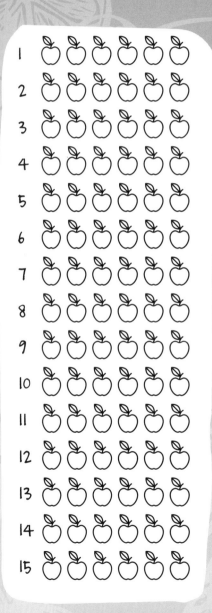

Water Tracker

One drop = one glass (400 ml)

1 ○○○○○○○○
2 ○○○○○○○○
3 ○○○○○○○○
4 ○○○○○○○○
5 ○○○○○○○○
6 ○○○○○○○○
7 ○○○○○○○○
8 ○○○○○○○○
9 ○○○○○○○○
10 ○○○○○○○○
11 ○○○○○○○○
12 ○○○○○○○○
13 ○○○○○○○○
14 ○○○○○○○○
15 ○○○○○○○○

16 ○○○○○○○○
17 ○○○○○○○○
18 ○○○○○○○○
19 ○○○○○○○○
20 ○○○○○○○○
21 ○○○○○○○○
22 ○○○○○○○○
23 ○○○○○○○○
24 ○○○○○○○○
25 ○○○○○○○○
26 ○○○○○○○○
27 ○○○○○○○○
28 ○○○○○○○○
29 ○○○○○○○○
30 ○○○○○○○○

Stress Tracker

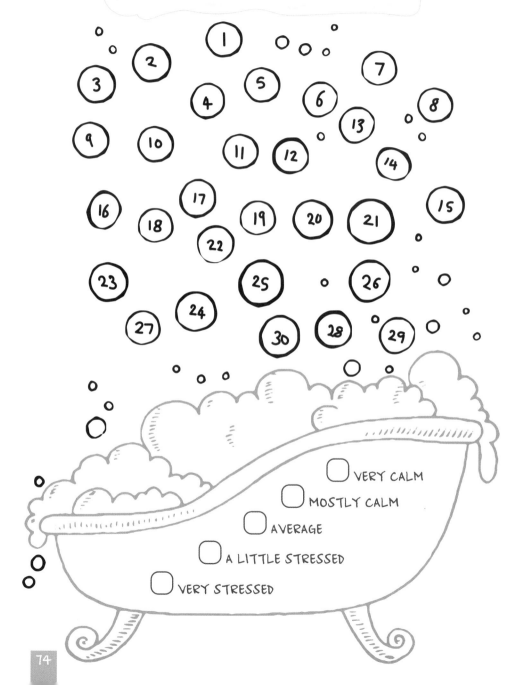

1 2 3 4 5 6 7 8 9 10 11 12 13 14 15 16 17 18 19 20 21 22 23 24 25 26 27 28 29 30

☐ VERY CALM
☐ MOSTLY CALM
☐ AVERAGE
☐ A LITTLE STRESSED
☐ VERY STRESSED

Working Out My Worries

Use this page to write down some of the things that you are worried about this month. Then think about ways you could overcome your worries, and write down some ideas you'd like to try out.

Things I'm worried about

_____

_____

_____

_____

How to overcome them

_____

_____

_____

_____

Sleep Tracker

○ FOUR HOURS OR FEWER   ○ FIVE HOURS   ○ SIX HOURS
○ SEVEN HOURS   ○ EIGHT HOURS   ○ NINE HOURS OR MORE

Calm Activity

HAPPY MEMORIES

Use this page to write down some happiest memories in your life, and read them whenever you need a reminder of all the things there are to be grateful for.

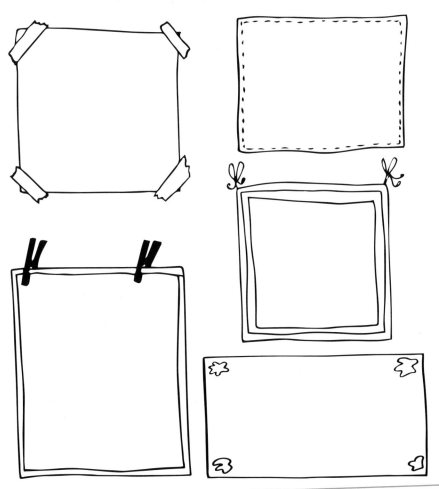

Wellness tracker

On each day this month, colour in one shape
according to how you feel.

KEY

◯ Great ◯ Good ◯ Average
◯ Poor ◯ Terrible

I am allowed
to slow down
and rest

Top Tips

SLOWING DOWN

Know Your Limits

In the busiest and most sociable time of the year, it's more important than ever that you recognize your own limits. Although it can be fun and exhilarating to pack your schedule with events, parties and gatherings, the reality is that time to yourself is still critical to your well-being. Take account of your boundaries when filling out your diary, and make sure you mark out some time for yourself.

Embrace JOMO

When all you see on social media is friends – and even strangers – having a wonderful time, it can be difficult not to feel like you're missing out on all the fun. But instead of letting FOMO get you down, try to embrace JOMO (the joy of missing out). Taking time to do what you want to do, and prioritizing your own needs, will bring you so much more happiness than working to others' schedules.

Exercise tracker

Use this page to log your levels of
activity over this month.

◯ ACTIVE   ◯ MODERATELY ACTIVE   ◯ REST DAY

Be healthy and take care of
yourself, but be happy with
the beautiful things that
make you, you.

BEYONCÉ

Five A Day Tracker

Each apple = one of your five
fruits or vegetables a day

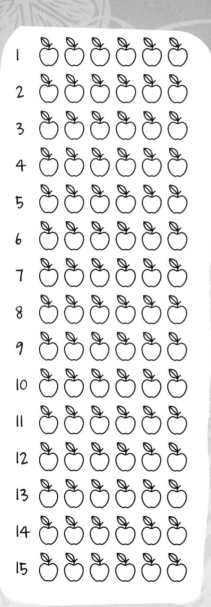

Water Tracker

One drop = one glass (400 ml)

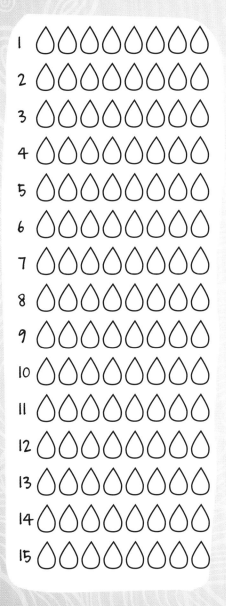

1 ◊◊◊◊◊◊◊◊
2 ◊◊◊◊◊◊◊◊
3 ◊◊◊◊◊◊◊◊
4 ◊◊◊◊◊◊◊◊
5 ◊◊◊◊◊◊◊◊
6 ◊◊◊◊◊◊◊◊
7 ◊◊◊◊◊◊◊◊
8 ◊◊◊◊◊◊◊◊
9 ◊◊◊◊◊◊◊◊
10 ◊◊◊◊◊◊◊◊
11 ◊◊◊◊◊◊◊◊
12 ◊◊◊◊◊◊◊◊
13 ◊◊◊◊◊◊◊◊
14 ◊◊◊◊◊◊◊◊
15 ◊◊◊◊◊◊◊◊

16 ◊◊◊◊◊◊◊◊
17 ◊◊◊◊◊◊◊◊
18 ◊◊◊◊◊◊◊◊
19 ◊◊◊◊◊◊◊◊
20 ◊◊◊◊◊◊◊◊
21 ◊◊◊◊◊◊◊◊
22 ◊◊◊◊◊◊◊◊
23 ◊◊◊◊◊◊◊◊
24 ◊◊◊◊◊◊◊◊
25 ◊◊◊◊◊◊◊◊
26 ◊◊◊◊◊◊◊◊
27 ◊◊◊◊◊◊◊◊
28 ◊◊◊◊◊◊◊◊
29 ◊◊◊◊◊◊◊◊
30 ◊◊◊◊◊◊◊◊
31 ◊◊◊◊◊◊◊◊

Stress Tracker

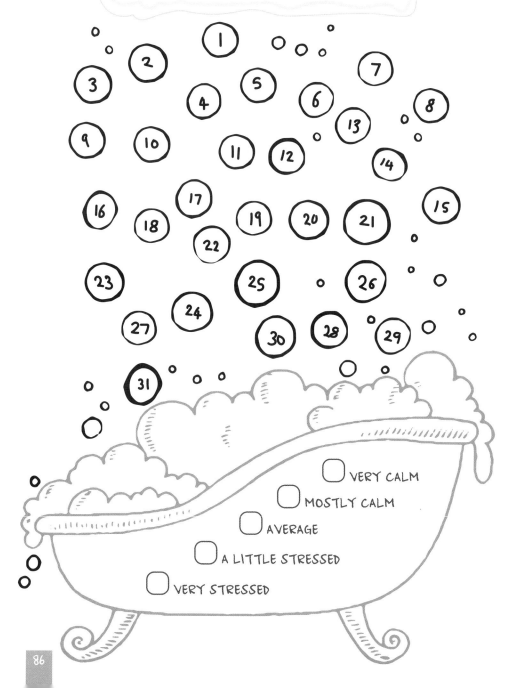

1 2 3 4 5 6 7 8 9 10 11 12 13 14 15 16 17 18 19 20 21 22 23 24 25 26 27 28 29 30 31

- ☐ VERY CALM
- ☐ MOSTLY CALM
- ☐ AVERAGE
- ☐ A LITTLE STRESSED
- ☐ VERY STRESSED

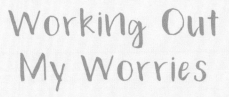

Working Out My Worries

Use this page to write down some of the things that you are worried about this month. Then think about ways you could overcome your worries, and write down some ideas you'd like to try out.

Things I'm worried about

_____

_____

_____

_____

How to overcome them

_____

_____

_____

_____

Sleep Tracker

FOUR HOURS OR FEWER   FIVE HOURS   SIX HOURS

SEVEN HOURS   EIGHT HOURS   NINE HOURS OR MORE

Calm Activity

YIN YOGA

Yin yoga is a slow-paced style of yoga, allowing more time to restore calm. Find a position where you feel comfortable and hold each of the below poses for three to five minutes. This practice is about being gentle with yourself and finding what feels good.

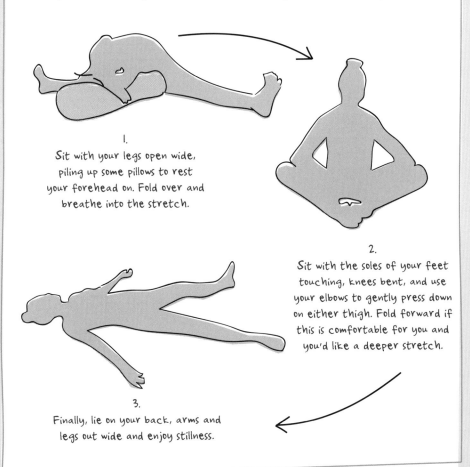

1.
Sit with your legs open wide, piling up some pillows to rest your forehead on. Fold over and breathe into the stretch.

2.
Sit with the soles of your feet touching, knees bent, and use your elbows to gently press down on either thigh. Fold forward if this is comfortable for you and you'd like a deeper stretch.

3.
Finally, lie on your back, arms and legs out wide and enjoy stillness.

Wellness tracker

On each day this month, colour in one shape
according to how you feel.

KEY

◯ Great ◯ Good ◯ Average
◯ Poor ◯ Terrible

I am comfortable
in my own skin and
radiate a beautiful,
healthy glow

Top Tips

TAKING CARE OF YOUR SKIN

Skincare as Self-Love

While inner beauty is what matters most, skincare plays an important part in us looking and feeling our best. Our skin tells a story about our health, so part of good skincare is looking after ourselves from the inside. That doesn't mean we should dispense with the cleansers and creams. Soothing rituals, such as massaging a facial oil into your skin, can also relax your mind and body, as well as help keep your skin soothed and moisturized.

Build a Skincare Routine

Not only will a regular skincare routine benefit our skin in the long term, but the fact that this process allows us to take a few minutes out of our day to focus on ourselves is also an act of self-love. Whether we use two products or ten, engaging in a skincare routine is beneficial to both our body and mind. Consider introducing a weekly deep cleanse, natural clay face mask or facial massage for some additional pampering!

Stay Hydrated

One of the biggest ways that we can ensure healthy body and skin is to keep ourselves hydrated. It is generally recommended that we drink six to eight glasses (around two litres) of fluid a day – ideally water.

Exercise tracker

Use this page to log your levels of activity over this month.

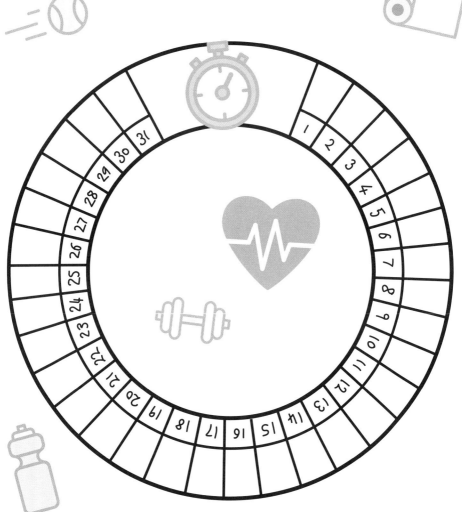

1 2 3 4 5 6 7 8 9 10 11 12 13 14 15 16 17 18 19 20 21 22 23 24 25 26 27 28 29 30 31

◯ ACTIVE   ◯ MODERATELY ACTIVE   ◯ REST DAY

Nourishing yourself in a
way that helps you blossom
in the direction you want
to go is attainable, and
you are worth the effort.

DEBORAH DAY

Five A Day Tracker

Each apple = one of your five
fruits or vegetables a day

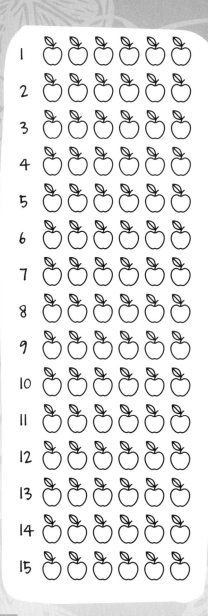

Water Tracker

One drop = one glass (400 ml)

1 ◊◊◊◊◊◊◊◊
2 ◊◊◊◊◊◊◊◊
3 ◊◊◊◊◊◊◊◊
4 ◊◊◊◊◊◊◊◊
5 ◊◊◊◊◊◊◊◊
6 ◊◊◊◊◊◊◊◊
7 ◊◊◊◊◊◊◊◊
8 ◊◊◊◊◊◊◊◊
9 ◊◊◊◊◊◊◊◊
10 ◊◊◊◊◊◊◊◊
11 ◊◊◊◊◊◊◊◊
12 ◊◊◊◊◊◊◊◊
13 ◊◊◊◊◊◊◊◊
14 ◊◊◊◊◊◊◊◊
15 ◊◊◊◊◊◊◊◊

16 ◊◊◊◊◊◊◊◊
17 ◊◊◊◊◊◊◊◊
18 ◊◊◊◊◊◊◊◊
19 ◊◊◊◊◊◊◊◊
20 ◊◊◊◊◊◊◊◊
21 ◊◊◊◊◊◊◊◊
22 ◊◊◊◊◊◊◊◊
23 ◊◊◊◊◊◊◊◊
24 ◊◊◊◊◊◊◊◊
25 ◊◊◊◊◊◊◊◊
26 ◊◊◊◊◊◊◊◊
27 ◊◊◊◊◊◊◊◊
28 ◊◊◊◊◊◊◊◊
29 ◊◊◊◊◊◊◊◊
30 ◊◊◊◊◊◊◊◊
31 ◊◊◊◊◊◊◊◊

Stress Tracker

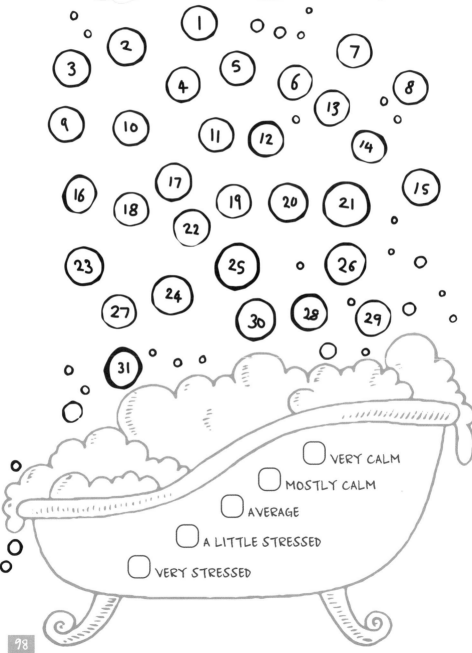

- VERY CALM
- MOSTLY CALM
- AVERAGE
- A LITTLE STRESSED
- VERY STRESSED

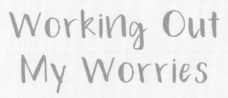

Working Out My Worries

Use this page to write down some of the things that you are worried about this month. Then think about ways you could overcome your worries, and write down some ideas you'd like to try out.

Things I'm worried about

_____

_____

_____

_____

How to overcome them

_____

_____

_____

_____

Sleep Tracker

- ☐ FOUR HOURS OR FEWER   ☐ FIVE HOURS   ☐ SIX HOURS
- ☐ SEVEN HOURS   ☐ EIGHT HOURS   ☐ NINE HOURS OR MORE

Calm Activity

MY PAMPER ROUTINE

In the circles below, write out each element of your ideal pamper routine. Fill out as many of the circles as you would like and draw in some arrows to indicate the order in which the steps should be carried out. Try to make this regime part of your daily — or weekly — routine.

Wellness tracker

On each day this month, colour in one shape according to how you feel.

KEY

⬜ Great ⬜ Good ⬜ Average
⬜ Poor ⬜ Terrible

I embrace
change and let
go of whatever
is holding
me back

Top Tips

COPING WITH CHANGE

Seasons of Life

Life is full of changes, but we only have to look to nature to see that change is natural, normal and necessary to growth. Whenever we feel stuck and fearful of the changes before us, perhaps we can learn something from the transformations of the natural world. Consider, for instance, whether a tough period in your life could be a way of making space for something new – just as winter is a necessary precursor of spring.

Letting Go

Before we can fully embrace change in our lives, we often have to let go of what has come before. Letting go not only liberates us from the weight of our past, but also gives us the freedom to fully embrace the present moment. The past cannot be altered, so lingering on it only serves to waste our time and our energy.

Exercise tracker

Use this page to log your levels of
activity over this month.

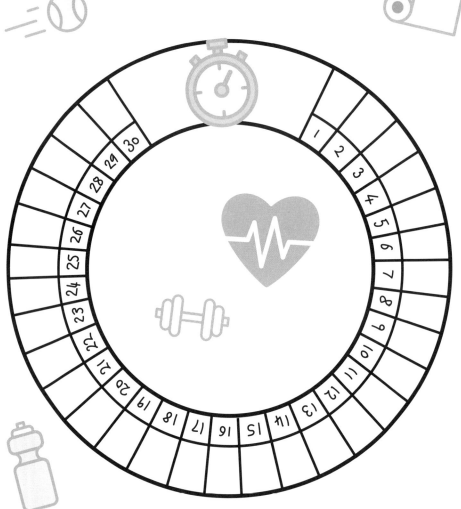

○ ACTIVE   ○ MODERATELY ACTIVE   ○ REST DAY

Trust that your soul has
a plan, and even if you
can't see it completely,
know that everything will
unfold as it is meant to.

DEEPAK CHOPRA

Five A Day Tracker

Each apple = one of your five
fruits or vegetables a day

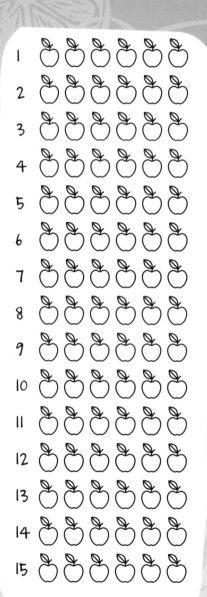

1
2
3
4
5
6
7
8
9
10
11
12
13
14
15

16
17
18
19
20
21
22
23
24
25
26
27
28
29
30

Water Tracker

One drop = one glass (400 ml)

1 ○○○○○○○○
2 ○○○○○○○○
3 ○○○○○○○○
4 ○○○○○○○○
5 ○○○○○○○○
6 ○○○○○○○○
7 ○○○○○○○○
8 ○○○○○○○○
9 ○○○○○○○○
10 ○○○○○○○○
11 ○○○○○○○○
12 ○○○○○○○○
13 ○○○○○○○○
14 ○○○○○○○○
15 ○○○○○○○○

16 ○○○○○○○○
17 ○○○○○○○○
18 ○○○○○○○○
19 ○○○○○○○○
20 ○○○○○○○○
21 ○○○○○○○○
22 ○○○○○○○○
23 ○○○○○○○○
24 ○○○○○○○○
25 ○○○○○○○○
26 ○○○○○○○○
27 ○○○○○○○○
28 ○○○○○○○○
29 ○○○○○○○○
30 ○○○○○○○○

Stress Tracker

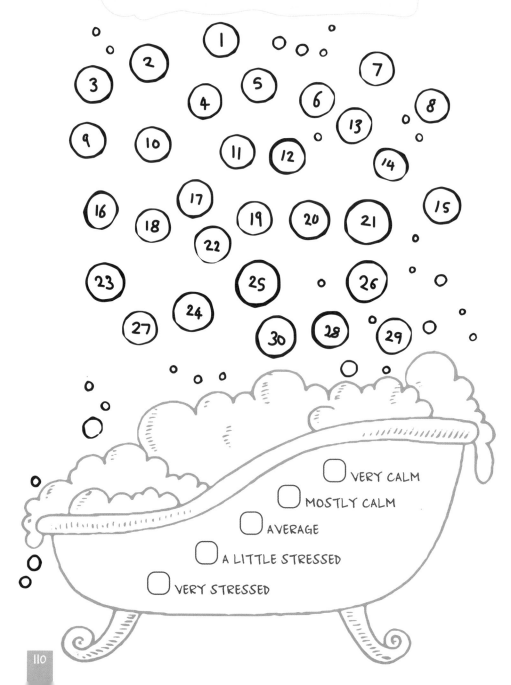

1 2 3 4 5 6 7 8 9 10 11 12 13 14 15 16 17 18 19 20 21 22 23 24 25 26 27 28 29 30

☐ VERY CALM
☐ MOSTLY CALM
☐ AVERAGE
☐ A LITTLE STRESSED
☐ VERY STRESSED

Working Out My Worries

Use this page to write down some of the things that you are worried about this month. Then think about ways you could overcome your worries, and write down some ideas you'd like to try out.

Things I'm worried about

_____
_____
_____
_____

How to overcome them

_____
_____
_____
_____

Sleep Tracker

☐ FOUR HOURS OR FEWER   ☐ FIVE HOURS   ☐ SIX HOURS
☐ SEVEN HOURS   ☐ EIGHT HOURS   ☐ NINE HOURS OR MORE

Calm Activity

WORD SEARCH

```
J  U  D  L  O  N  N  H  U  I  P  M  C  P  T
Z  P  Q  W  A  J  O  P  M  C  M  M  H  W  Z
B  B  P  T  Z  N  I  H  R  Y  R  N  A  O  K
Q  Q  U  B  E  W  T  W  T  O  A  U  N  L  P
X  R  C  W  M  C  I  K  F  R  T  W  G  F  I
E  Y  W  N  G  K  S  S  S  P  A  T  E  G  M
O  G  X  N  U  R  N  G  Q  E  Q  E  M  W  W
O  B  L  O  J  A  A  Y  X  X  J  G  R  A  D
S  U  Q  M  R  B  R  J  E  L  U  T  K  X  D
K  E  M  T  R  C  T  E  M  W  E  I  G  H  Z
T  P  A  L  A  N  D  S  C  A  P  E  U  D  N
U  W  F  S  S  G  O  D  I  N  O  T  Q  L  T
S  O  O  Q  O  J  R  Z  K  K  Z  D  Y  C  I
D  H  J  V  C  N  I  M  O  D  S  I  W  S  R
Z  N  R  F  L  H  S  H  B  B  C  Z  T  V  K
```

CHANGE	EARTH	FLOW
LANDSCAPE	NATURE	SEASONS
TRANSFORM	TRANSITION	WISDOM

Wellness tracker

On each day this month, colour in one shape
according to how you feel.

KEY

◯ Great ◯ Good ◯ Average
◯ Poor ◯ Terrible

I deserve to
be happy and
celebrate my
successes

Top Tips

FINDING HAPPINESS

Happiness is Key

Happiness is fundamental to our well-being, since it has such a big impact on our mental and physical health. Countless studies have shown that being happy promotes a healthy lifestyle, as well as helping to combat stress, boosting your immune system and increasing your overall life expectancy – so there's a lot to smile about!

Create a "Joy Jar"

Try to keep a track of your most joyful moments this month. Each time something makes you laugh out loud, or you find yourself in especially good spirits, write a note of what it was that made you so happy.

Place each of your notes in a container labelled "Joy Jar", and revisit your happy moments as often as you like. You might be surprised by how much happiness you already have in your life.

Recite Affirmations

Affirmations are statements or propositions that you tell yourself as if they are true. Studies have shown that those who recite positive affirmations have increased self-worth and feel more validated. Try reciting some of the affirmations in this book to yourself regularly to help promote positive thinking.

Exercise tracker

Use this page to log your levels of
activity over this month.

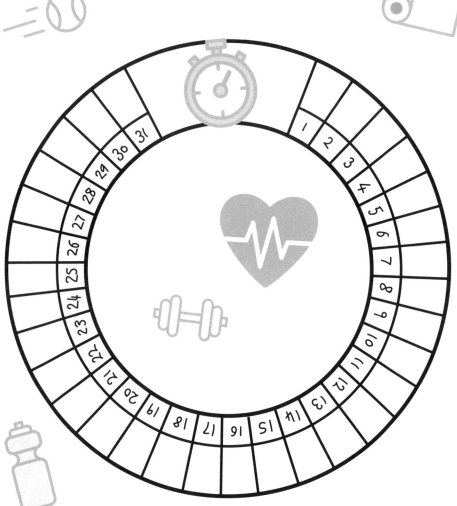

◯ ACTIVE   ◯ MODERATELY ACTIVE   ◯ REST DAY

Joy comes to us in
ordinary moments. We
risk missing out when
we get too busy chasing
down the extraordinary.

BRENÉ BROWN

Five A Day Tracker

Each apple = one of your five
fruits or vegetables a day

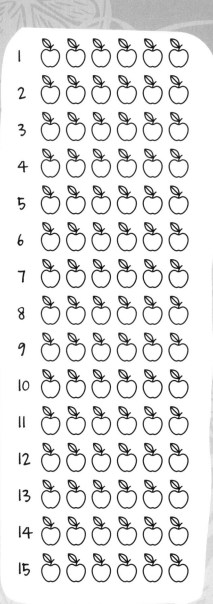

1
2
3
4
5
6
7
8
9
10
11
12
13
14
15

16
17
18
19
20
21
22
23
24
25
26
27
28
29
30
31

Water Tracker

One drop = one glass (400 ml)

1 ◌◌◌◌◌◌◌◌
2 ◌◌◌◌◌◌◌◌
3 ◌◌◌◌◌◌◌◌
4 ◌◌◌◌◌◌◌◌
5 ◌◌◌◌◌◌◌◌
6 ◌◌◌◌◌◌◌◌
7 ◌◌◌◌◌◌◌◌
8 ◌◌◌◌◌◌◌◌
9 ◌◌◌◌◌◌◌◌
10 ◌◌◌◌◌◌◌◌
11 ◌◌◌◌◌◌◌◌
12 ◌◌◌◌◌◌◌◌
13 ◌◌◌◌◌◌◌◌
14 ◌◌◌◌◌◌◌◌
15 ◌◌◌◌◌◌◌◌

16 ◌◌◌◌◌◌◌◌
17 ◌◌◌◌◌◌◌◌
18 ◌◌◌◌◌◌◌◌
19 ◌◌◌◌◌◌◌◌
20 ◌◌◌◌◌◌◌◌
21 ◌◌◌◌◌◌◌◌
22 ◌◌◌◌◌◌◌◌
23 ◌◌◌◌◌◌◌◌
24 ◌◌◌◌◌◌◌◌
25 ◌◌◌◌◌◌◌◌
26 ◌◌◌◌◌◌◌◌
27 ◌◌◌◌◌◌◌◌
28 ◌◌◌◌◌◌◌◌
29 ◌◌◌◌◌◌◌◌
30 ◌◌◌◌◌◌◌◌
31 ◌◌◌◌◌◌◌◌

Stress Tracker

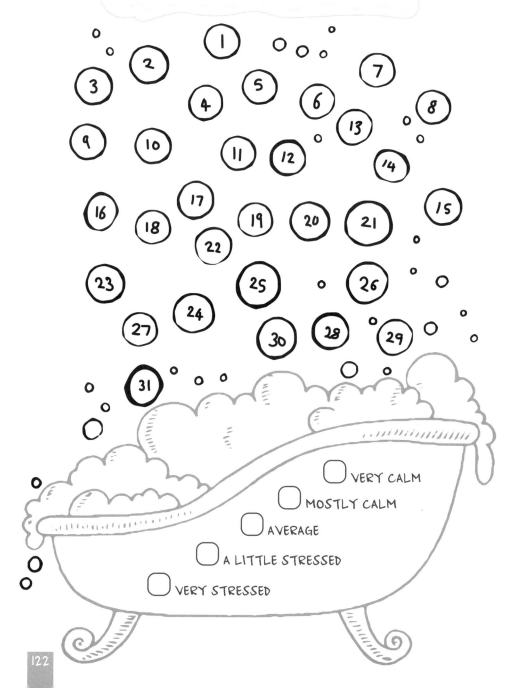

1 2 3 4 5 6 7 8 9 10 11 12 13 14 15 16 17 18 19 20 21 22 23 24 25 26 27 28 29 30 31

☐ VERY CALM
☐ MOSTLY CALM
☐ AVERAGE
☐ A LITTLE STRESSED
☐ VERY STRESSED

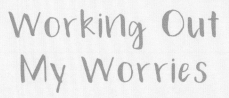

Working Out My Worries

Use this page to write down some of the things that you are worried about this month. Then think about ways you could overcome your worries, and write down some ideas you'd like to try out.

Things I'm worried about

_____

_____

_____

_____

How to overcome them

_____

_____

_____

_____

Sleep Tracker

- FOUR HOURS OR FEWER
- FIVE HOURS
- SIX HOURS
- SEVEN HOURS
- EIGHT HOURS
- NINE HOURS OR MORE

Calm Activity

SPOT THE DIFFERENCE

When we search for happiness, we often find that it's already right in front of us. Try to spot the ten differences between these two joyful pictures.

Wellness tracker

On each day this month, colour in one shape according to how you feel.

KEY

◯ Great ◯ Good ◯ Average
◯ Poor ◯ Terrible

I exhale
stress and I
inhale calm

Top Tips

MEDITATING

Build Your Awareness

Mindfulness meditation is about focusing on the present moment, and about paying attention to your breath; it does not mean that you have to fully empty your brain of thoughts, or that you have failed if your mind wanders for a few seconds. Mindfulness meditation is all about building awareness, and it can help us to reduce stress, improve our focus and find some inner peace.

Learning to Meditate

Follow the steps below to try out some mindfulness meditation:

- Find a place where you can sit comfortably, and close your eyes.

- Focus on your connection to the earth and the feeling of your body against the ground.

- Notice the natural rhythm of your breath.

- Tune into the sounds around you, and then bring your awareness to the sounds that you are making as you breathe.

- Observe your thoughts, coming and going. Don't push them away, but don't focus on them either – simply let them drift in and out of your mind.

- Bring your awareness back to your breath.

- When you're ready, take a final deep breath and slowly open your eyes.

- Notice how your body feels after this short practice.

Exercise tracker

Use this page to log your levels of
activity over this month.

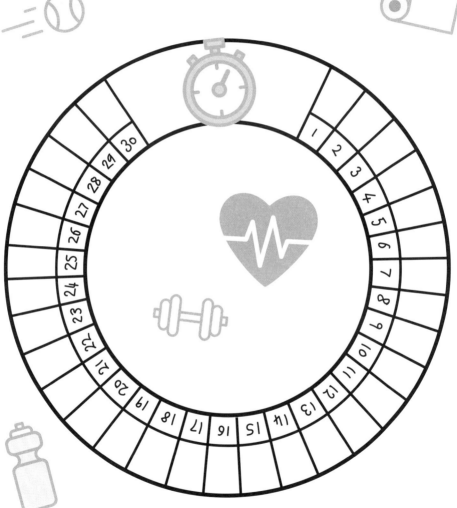

1 2 3 4 5 6 7 8 9 10 11 12 13 14 15 16 17 18 19 20 21 22 23 24 25 26 27 28 29 30

○ ACTIVE   ○ MODERATELY ACTIVE   ○ REST DAY

To a mind that is still, the whole universe surrenders.

LAO TZU

Five A Day Tracker

Each apple = one of your five
fruits or vegetables a day

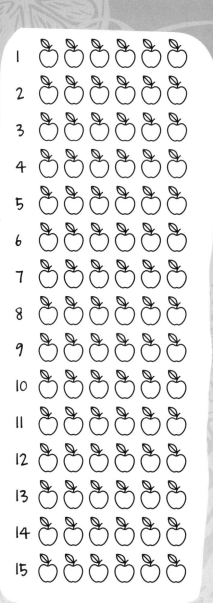

Water Tracker

One drop = one glass (400 ml)

1 ◊◊◊◊◊◊◊◊
2 ◊◊◊◊◊◊◊◊
3 ◊◊◊◊◊◊◊◊
4 ◊◊◊◊◊◊◊◊
5 ◊◊◊◊◊◊◊◊
6 ◊◊◊◊◊◊◊◊
7 ◊◊◊◊◊◊◊◊
8 ◊◊◊◊◊◊◊◊
9 ◊◊◊◊◊◊◊◊
10 ◊◊◊◊◊◊◊◊
11 ◊◊◊◊◊◊◊◊
12 ◊◊◊◊◊◊◊◊
13 ◊◊◊◊◊◊◊◊
14 ◊◊◊◊◊◊◊◊
15 ◊◊◊◊◊◊◊◊

16 ◊◊◊◊◊◊◊◊
17 ◊◊◊◊◊◊◊◊
18 ◊◊◊◊◊◊◊◊
19 ◊◊◊◊◊◊◊◊
20 ◊◊◊◊◊◊◊◊
21 ◊◊◊◊◊◊◊◊
22 ◊◊◊◊◊◊◊◊
23 ◊◊◊◊◊◊◊◊
24 ◊◊◊◊◊◊◊◊
25 ◊◊◊◊◊◊◊◊
26 ◊◊◊◊◊◊◊◊
27 ◊◊◊◊◊◊◊◊
28 ◊◊◊◊◊◊◊◊
29 ◊◊◊◊◊◊◊◊
30 ◊◊◊◊◊◊◊◊

Stress Tracker

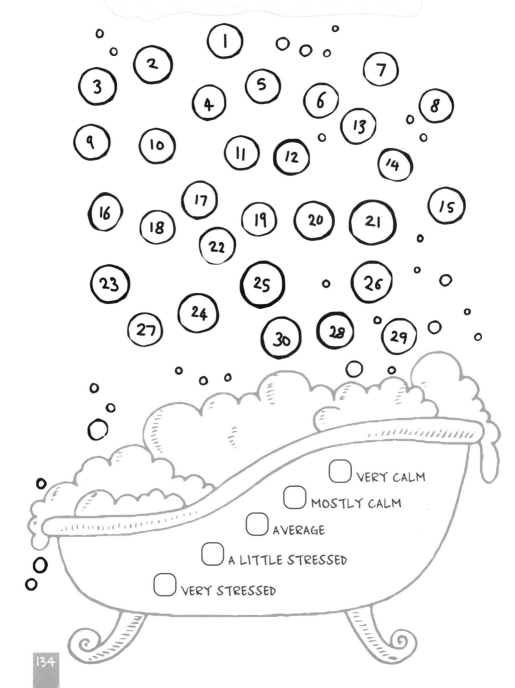

☐ VERY CALM

☐ MOSTLY CALM

☐ AVERAGE

☐ A LITTLE STRESSED

☐ VERY STRESSED

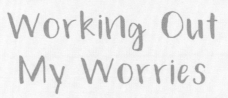

Working Out My Worries

Use this page to write down some of the things that you are worried about this month. Then think about ways you could overcome your worries, and write down some ideas you'd like to try out.

Things I'm worried about

_____

_____

_____

_____

How to overcome them

_____

_____

_____

_____

Sleep Tracker

- ☐ FOUR HOURS OR FEWER
- ☐ FIVE HOURS
- ☐ SIX HOURS
- ☐ SEVEN HOURS
- ☐ EIGHT HOURS
- ☐ NINE HOURS OR MORE

Calm Activity

MINDFUL COLOURING

Colouring has been shown to help us focus
on the present moment, as well as help
to reduce feelings of stress and anxiety.
Colour the picture below for a dose of calm.

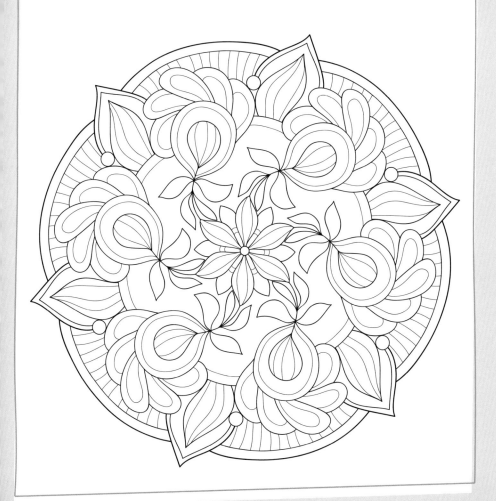

Wellness tracker

On each day this month, colour in one shape
according to how you feel.

KEY

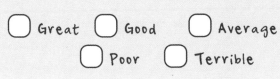

◯ Great   ◯ Good   ◯ Average
          ◯ Poor   ◯ Terrible

I respect the
rhythms of my
body and I welcome
the tranquillity
of sleep

Top Tips

SLEEPING WELL

Respect Your Sleep Cycle

Sleep is very important for our well-being, so we should always make sure to get the most out of our rest. Although there is no exact science to how much sleep you need, an adult should be getting an average of seven to nine hours of sleep per night. It's important that we listen to our body when it comes to sleep; if you feel very tired a lot of the time, consider whether you could improve the length and/or quality of your sleep.

Put Down Your Gadgets

Phone, tablet and laptop screens all emit blue light, which can interfere with our circadian rhythm. Make sure you turn off (or put away) technology at least 30 minutes before you go to sleep to avoid stimulating your body and mind. Try instead to read a book or write in a diary before you go to sleep to promote rest and relaxation.

Keep it Cool

For an optimal night's sleep, the temperature of your bedroom should be between 16 and 19°C, so avoid leaving the heating on at night. If possible, leave a window open for additional ventilation to help you stay cool.

Exercise tracker

Use this page to log your levels of activity over this month.

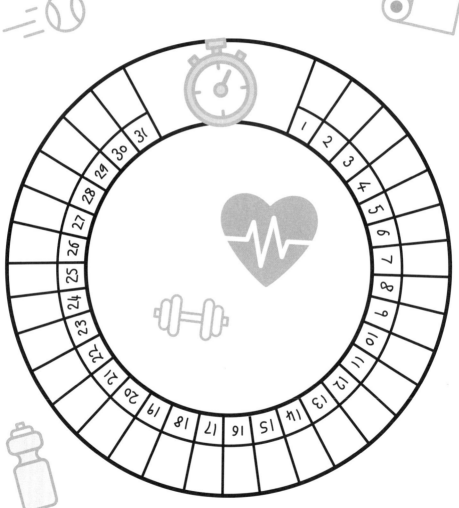

1 2 3 4 5 6 7 8 9 10 11 12 13 14 15 16 17 18 19 20 21 22 23 24 25 26 27 28 29 30 31

⬭ ACTIVE ⬭ MODERATELY ACTIVE ⬭ REST DAY

I love to sleep. When I'm rested, I'm at my best.

HALLE BERRY

Five A Day Tracker

Each apple = one of your five
fruits or vegetables a day

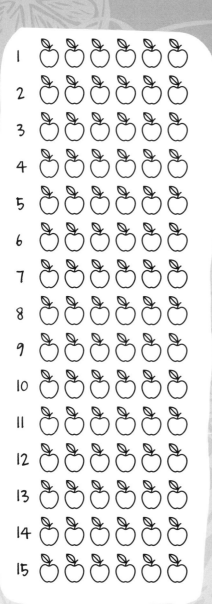

Water Tracker

One drop = one glass (400 ml)

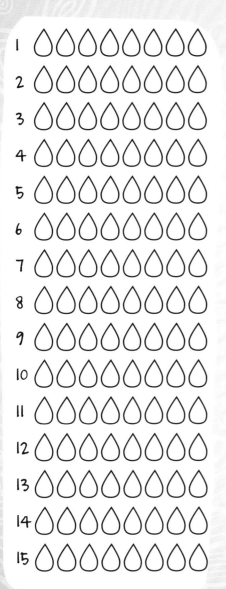

1 ⬯⬯⬯⬯⬯⬯⬯⬯
2 ⬯⬯⬯⬯⬯⬯⬯⬯
3 ⬯⬯⬯⬯⬯⬯⬯⬯
4 ⬯⬯⬯⬯⬯⬯⬯⬯
5 ⬯⬯⬯⬯⬯⬯⬯⬯
6 ⬯⬯⬯⬯⬯⬯⬯⬯
7 ⬯⬯⬯⬯⬯⬯⬯⬯
8 ⬯⬯⬯⬯⬯⬯⬯⬯
9 ⬯⬯⬯⬯⬯⬯⬯⬯
10 ⬯⬯⬯⬯⬯⬯⬯⬯
11 ⬯⬯⬯⬯⬯⬯⬯⬯
12 ⬯⬯⬯⬯⬯⬯⬯⬯
13 ⬯⬯⬯⬯⬯⬯⬯⬯
14 ⬯⬯⬯⬯⬯⬯⬯⬯
15 ⬯⬯⬯⬯⬯⬯⬯⬯

16 ⬯⬯⬯⬯⬯⬯⬯⬯
17 ⬯⬯⬯⬯⬯⬯⬯⬯
18 ⬯⬯⬯⬯⬯⬯⬯⬯
19 ⬯⬯⬯⬯⬯⬯⬯⬯
20 ⬯⬯⬯⬯⬯⬯⬯⬯
21 ⬯⬯⬯⬯⬯⬯⬯⬯
22 ⬯⬯⬯⬯⬯⬯⬯⬯
23 ⬯⬯⬯⬯⬯⬯⬯⬯
24 ⬯⬯⬯⬯⬯⬯⬯⬯
25 ⬯⬯⬯⬯⬯⬯⬯⬯
26 ⬯⬯⬯⬯⬯⬯⬯⬯
27 ⬯⬯⬯⬯⬯⬯⬯⬯
28 ⬯⬯⬯⬯⬯⬯⬯⬯
29 ⬯⬯⬯⬯⬯⬯⬯⬯
30 ⬯⬯⬯⬯⬯⬯⬯⬯
31 ⬯⬯⬯⬯⬯⬯⬯⬯

Stress Tracker

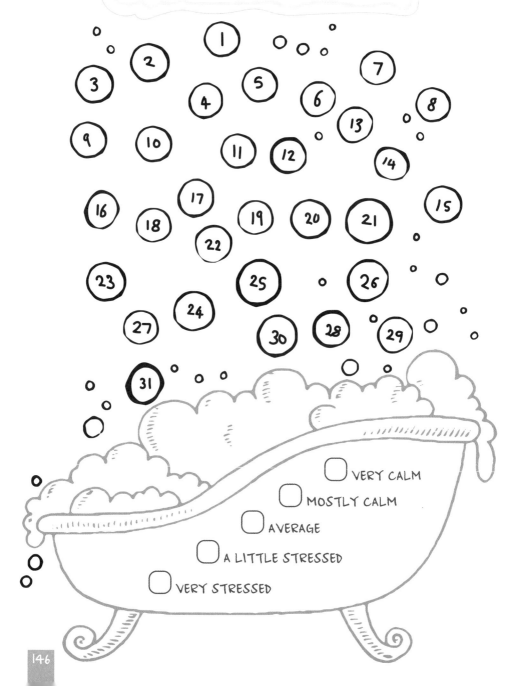

1 2 3 4 5 6 7 8 9 10 11 12 13 14 15 16 17 18 19 20 21 22 23 24 25 26 27 28 29 30 31

☐ VERY CALM

☐ MOSTLY CALM

☐ AVERAGE

☐ A LITTLE STRESSED

☐ VERY STRESSED

Working Out My Worries

Use this page to write down some of the things that you are worried about this month. Then think about ways you could overcome your worries, and write down some ideas you'd like to try out.

Things I'm worried about

_____

_____

_____

_____

How to overcome them

_____

_____

_____

_____

Sleep Tracker

☐ FOUR HOURS OR FEWER ☐ FIVE HOURS ☐ SIX HOURS

☐ SEVEN HOURS ☐ EIGHT HOURS ☐ NINE HOURS OR MORE

Calm Activity

DREAM DIARY

Use this page to note down any dreams that you'd like
to remember. Can you find any meaning in them?

He who lives in
harmony with himself
lives in harmony
with the universe.

ANONYMOUS

Conclusion

Congratulations – you've now been on your wellness journey for a whole year!

Before you start thinking about next year, take a moment to pause and reflect on all that you have learnt so far, and take a look back over the last 12 months to appreciate your journey. What has changed in your outlook? How do you want to continue?

The awareness you have developed by using this journal will continue to be valuable to you in your future, so take the lessons you have learned from this book and apply them to the rest your life. By now, daily reflection on your mood, sleep and behaviours should come naturally to you, so keep this as part of your routine if you can.

Hopefully this book has given you the space to reflect, and has provided you with insight so that you know how to continue your journey with a better understanding of your mental and physical well-being.

Answers

Page 41

Page 113

J	U	D	L	O	N	N	H	U	I	P	M	C	P	T
Z	P	Q	W	A	J	O	P	M	C	M	M	H	W	Z
B	B	P	T	Z	N	I	H	R	Y	R	N	A	O	K
Q	Q	U	B	E	W	T	W	T	O	A	U	N	L	P
X	R	C	W	M	C	I	K	F	R	T	W	G	F	I
E	Y	W	N	G	K	S	S	S	P	A	T	E	G	M
O	G	X	N	U	R	N	G	Q	E	Q	E	M	W	W
O	B	L	O	J	A	A	Y	X	X	J	G	R	A	D
S	U	Q	M	R	B	R	J	E	L	U	T	K	X	D
K	E	M	T	R	C	T	E	M	W	E	I	G	H	Z
T	P	A	L	A	N	D	S	C	A	P	E	U	D	N
U	W	F	S	S	G	O	D	I	N	O	T	Q	L	T
S	O	O	Q	O	J	R	Z	K	K	Z	D	Y	C	I
D	H	J	V	C	N	I	M	O	D	S	I	W	S	R
Z	N	R	F	L	H	S	H	B	B	C	Z	T	V	K

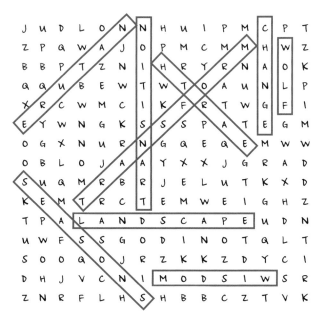

Page 125

Notes

Use this space to reflect on your
de-stressing journey so far.

Image credits

p.1 – background © HJ_Studio/Shutterstock.com; leaves © Wanchana365/Shutterstock.com

pp.6–7 – sun icons © AllNikArt/Shutterstock.com

pp. 9, 21, 33, 45, 57, 69, 81, 93, 105, 117, 129, 141 – background © antadi1332/Shutterstock.com

pp.10, 22, 34, 46, 58, 70, 82, 94, 106, 118, 130, 142 – sports icons © Shirstok/Shutterstock.com

pp.12, 24, 36, 48, 60, 72, 84, 96, 108, 120, 132, 144 – background © Matisson_ART/Shutterstock.com

pp.13, 25, 37, 49, 61, 73, 85, 97, 109, 11, 133, 145 – background © natsa/Shutterstock.com

pp.14, 26, 38, 50, 62, 74, 86, 98, 110, 122, 134, 146 – bathtub © N_Melanchenko/Shutterstock.com

pp.15, 27, 39, 51, 63, 75, 87, 99, 111, 123, 135, 147 – background © Mariia Sutyrina/Shutterstock.com

pp.16, 28, 40, 52, 64, 76, 88, 100, 112, 124, 136, 148 – sleep icons © Minur/Shutterstock.com

pp.18–19, 160 – flowers © Danussa/Shutterstock.com

p.29 – hearts © Omnart/Shutterstock.com

pp.30–31 – feathers © Maaike Boot/Shutterstock.com

pp.41, 152 – heart maze © PlatypusMi86/Shutterstock.com

pp.42–43 – balloons © Antonio Baranessku/Shutterstock.com

p.53 – music icons © Alexander Lysenko/Shutterstock.com

pp.54–55 – fish © xenia_ok/Shutterstock.com

pp.66–67 – strawberries © IRINA SHI/Shutterstock.com

p.77 – frames © Tsaranna/Shutterstock.com

pp.78–79 – leaves © Hulinska Yevheniia/Shutterstock.com

p.89 – top and middle yoga poses © Yaroslavna Zemtsova/
Shutterstock.com

p.89 – bottom yoga pose © Babkina Svetlana/Shutterstock.com

pp.90–91 – birds © Kolesnikov Vladimir/Shutterstock.com

p.101 – circles © Artishok/Shutterstock.com

pp.102–103 – drops © Dmitry Lampy/Shutterstock.com

pp.114–115 – poppies © M_Morozova/Shutterstock.com

pp.125, 153 – dreamcatcher © Ira Mukti/Shutterstock.com

pp.126–127 – lemons © orangeberry/Shutterstock.com

p.137 – mandala © Nonuzza/Shutterstock.com

pp.138–139 – hearts © Giamportone/Shutterstock.com

p.149 – bubbles © nikiteev_konstantin/Shutterstock.com

If you're interested in finding out more
about our books, find us on Facebook
at Summersdale Publishers and follow us
on Twitter at @Summersdale.

Thanks very much for buying this
Summersdale book.

www.summersdale.com